MOMMY,
CAN I HAVE THAT?

Allergy Friendly Recipes
The Whole Family Will Enjoy.
Egg Free, Dairy Free, Peanut Free, Tree Nut Free

Elizabeth Cosgrove Feeney

NFB
<<<>>>
Buffalo, NY

Printed in the United States of America

Feeney, Elizabeth Cosgrove

Mommy, Can I have That? Allergy Friendly Recipes the Whole Family Will Enjoy. Egg Free, Dairy Free, Peanut Free, Tree Nut Free/ 1st Edition

ISBN: 978-0692314722 (Black and White Version)

1. Cooking 2. Allergy Free 3. Dairy Free   4. Recipes 5. Nonfiction
1. Title

No Frills Buffalo Press
119 Dorchester Buffalo, New York 14213

For more information visit nofrillsbuffalo.com

This book is dedicated to the parents of kids with food allergies. It is a rough road sometimes. I hope this book helps to make the world of food allergies a little simpler, a little less scary and a whole lot tastier!

TABLE OF CONTENTS

INTRODUCTION

I was thrown into this allergy free world and my head was spinning. I remember I cried all the way home from the doctor's office. I didn't know what he was going eat or snack on. I thought, "Oh my goodness, he can't have anything!!" But I have come to learn that that is the farthest thing from the truth.

I have done years of reading and talking to people and more reading. I have tried so many recipes and I have actually thrown them out. I thought they would be great, but they tasted like poison! I am not a chef by any stretch of the imagination. I am an ordinary stay at home mom who just wants to make tasty food for her family that everyone can enjoy. I would make certain allergy friendly recipes that for Logan, but I expected no one else would eat. That got old really fast.

I decided to hone in on certain recipes from my grandma, and from some of her old cookbooks and switch ingredients to make them allergy friendly. I have talked to people in grocery stores, health food stores, and read a lot on the internet about allergy friendly diets, vegan diets, and all kinds of fantastic recipes that can easily be switched into allergy friendly recipes.

One major thing that has greatly improved over the last few years is the packaging of products. The top 8 allergens are listed in bold after the ingredient section if present in the product. Later I will give you some advice on how to read product labels and figure out if that product is safe for you.

Another issue is the severity of the allergy you are dealing with. My son cannot have a product if the allergen is present in the product or if it is made in a facility that produces that product.

I have learned that a factory produces many items and many of these products can be produced on the same machinery. Sometimes they clean the belt, but not the machine or vice versa. Every factory is different and you never know about the cross contamination, but you just can't take that chance. But some allergy kids I know can have things that don't contain the allergen, but are made in a facility with one. Before you feed someone who has an allergy, make sure you know what their situation is.

This book is all about making recipes with everyday ingredients found in your kitchen without spending about $30 to make a pan of brownies! I have worked really hard to find recipes that use regular everyday ingredients.

Some of these recipes have specific allergic friendly ingredients, but I will tell you where to find them in the store. This was actually a big issue for me early on in my allergy free journey. I didn't know where to find certain allergy friendly ingredients for the recipes I was trying to make. So I worked to make recipes that didn't have so many complicated and expensive ingredients. I simply couldn't afford some of the products the recipes were calling for.

I actually would spend hours of time in the grocery store reading labels in the regular store, not the organic section. So I would pick an aisle per week and read almost every label to see what products are safe and which are not. I actually was shocked to learn all the products that are safe for Logan. One of my biggest pieces of advice for living with food allergies is to read, read, read.

I read all the time. Things are constantly changing and it is so important to read. Read labels constantly because something that could have been safe a month ago may not be safe anymore. Things change in the factories and the cross contamination of a certain product can always change. Another advantage of reading is you never know what you will be able to eat! In all of my experience in cooking and buying allergy friendly products for my son, the greatest lesson I have learned is you never know what they are going to be able to have. Some products really surprise you, and they can have them and on the flip side something you totally assume they can have is not allergy free.

Restaurants are also getting on the allergy friendly wagon. There are many places you can go to that have allergen identifying menus at the waitress stand. They list all the menu items and whether they contain any of the top 8 allergens. The problem is the overwhelming cross contamination that occurs in a restaurant. You can never be sure what allergen has crossed the path of your food. A lot of the time the restaurant will use the same oil to cook all different kinds of foods and that is where a lot of the cross contamination comes from.

Another very scary endeavor for an allergy parent is the idea of taking a vacation. The horror of going to a hotel, and constantly eating in a restaurant, or if there are stores near the vacation spot that will have the items your person can eat. How much food can you actually bring with you so they can eat safely. The worries go on and on. It is emotionally exhausting and nerve-wracking.

We have gone on three vacations in the past few years where the wait staff and restaurants go out of their way to make us feel comfortable with my child eating there. There is something about the way they answer your questions that let you know they know what they are doing. As an allergy parent, you know what I am talking about! Nothing is worse than that blank stare when the server is not sure what you are talking about,on one occasion they didn't think butter is dairy! Ahhh yikes! But like I say all the time, if you are not in this situation everyday it is really hard to get a handle on all that it involves and it is really easy to make a mistake. But as an allergy parent you cannot take that chance with your person getting sick or stopping breathing.

In those restaurants, when you tell your server that someone in the group has a food allergy, the chef will actually come out and talk to you and give you options for their order. It is really cool because we all know that is a pretty big deal. My favorite thing about it is that these people are very knowledgeable and it makes you very comfortable that there will not be any mistakes because of a lack of understanding food allergies.

Another really great thing I have learned in my journey is how much you can learn just by asking questions.

I hope you enjoy the recipes in this book. I have worked very hard at making these recipes delicious and everyone in your family will eat.

Reading A Label

I will explain how to properly read a label. As I stated, reading a label is one of the most important aspects of being an allergy mom. Friends sometimes call me when they have to bring in a snack for their child's school and they don't know if the product is safe.

Most product labels have the top 8 allergens in bold letters underneath the ingredient list. Those are wheat, soy, eggs, dairy, peanut, tree nuts, shellfish and fish.

Another important issue for your allergy person is to find out whether they are able to eat foods that while they do not contain the allergen, are made or processed in a facility that manufactures that allergen. My son cannot eat anything that has the allergen or is processed in a facility that manufactures the allergen. However some people can eat things that do not contain the allergen but are processed in a facility where that allergen is made.

Here are a couple of examples of labels. The top is an example of a label that states the product is manufactured in a facility with the allergens listed. The bottom has allergens are listed in bold.

INGREDIENTS: Wheat Flour, Bleached, Enriched, Bromated (Wheat Flour, Malted Barley Flour, Niacin, Reduced Iron, Potassium Bromate, Thiamine Mononitrate, Riboflavin and Folic Acid), Water, Yeast, Contains 2% or less of: Vinegar, Ascorbic Acid, Azodicarbonamide, Calcium Sulfate, Calcium Propionate (To Preserve Freshness), DATEM, Enzymes, L-cysteine, Salt, Vegetable Shortening (Partially Hydrogenated Soybean, Cottonseed and Canola Oils, Mono- & Diglycerides), Sesame and Poppy Seeds when apparent

PROCESSED IN A FACILITY THAT USES: EGGS, MILK AND SOY. CONTAINS: WHEAT

INGREDIENTS: ENRICHED FLOUR (WHEAT FLOUR, ENZYME, NIACIN, REDUCED IRON, THIAMINE MONONITRATE, RIBOFLAVIN, FOLIC ACID), WATER, SUGAR, LIQUID SUGAR (SUGAR, WATER), BUTTER (PASTEURIZED CREAM, SALT), EGGS, CONTAINS LESS THAN 2% OF EACH OF THE FOLLOWING: YEAST, POTATO FLOUR, WHEY, NONFAT MILK, SALT, DATEM, SOY FLOUR, YELLOW CORN FLOUR, SODIUM STEAROYL LACTYLATE, INACTIVE YEAST, WHEAT GLUTEN, SORBIC ACID PRESERVATIVE, MONOCALCIUM PHOSPHATE, WHEAT FLOUR, CALCIUM SULFATE, SODIUM SILICOALUMINATE, AMMONIUM SULFATE, ASCORBIC ACID ADDED AS A DOUGH CONDITIONER, WHEAT STARCH, SORBITAN MONOSTEARATE, MONO- & DIGLYCERIDES, ENZYMES, CALCIUM SILICATE, MICROCRYSTALLINE CELLULOSE.
CONTAINS: WHEAT, MILK, EGGS, SOY.

This label on the top is for a dairy free ice cream sandwich. On this label the different sections of the product are listed separately. For instance the wafer ingredients are separate from the non-dairy frozen section.

The label on the bottom lists the ingredients and how they may contain another allergen.

The biggest thing with labels is read, read, read.

INGREDIENTS: NON-DAIRY FROZEN DESSERT [ORGANIC COCONUT MILK (WATER, ORGANIC COCONUT CREAM), ORGANIC AGAVE SYRUP, CHICORY ROOT EXTRACT, CAROB BEAN GUM, GUAR GUM, VANILLA EXTRACT, NATURAL FLAVOR, VANILLA BEAN SPECKS], **WAFER** (WHEAT FLOUR, DRIED CANE SYRUP, PALM OIL, BROWN RICE SYRUP, CARAMEL COLOR, BAKING SODA, COCOA, CANOLA LECITHIN, SALT, NATURAL VANILLA FLAVOR).

ALLERGEN INFORMATION: We apply strict quality control measures in an effort to prevent contamination by undeclared food allergens. To assure our preventive measures are effective, we sample test our products for the presence of dairy, gluten, peanut, soy and tree nut allergens using state of the art testing methods. To learn more about our allergen prevention program visit us at SoDeliciousDairyFree.com.

CONTAINS: COCONUT, GLUTEN

Ingredients: Sugar, corn flour blend (whole grain yellow corn flour, degerminated yellow corn flour), wheat flour, whole grain oat flour, oat fiber, modified corn starch, contains 2% or less of corn syrup, dextrose, natural and artificial flavor, partially hydrogenated vegetable oil (coconut, soybean and/or cottonseed), soluble corn fiber, salt, gelatin, sodium hexametaphosphate, yellow 5, red 40, blue 2, yellow 6, blue 1, turmeric color, annatto color, BHT for freshness.

Vitamins and Minerals: Vitamin C (sodium ascorbate and ascorbic acid), niacinamide, reduced iron, zinc oxide, vitamin B_6 (pyridoxine hydrochloride), vitamin B_2 (riboflavin), vitamin B_1 (thiamin hydrochloride), vitamin A palmitate, folic acid, vitamin D, vitamin B_{12}.

CONTAINS WHEAT INGREDIENTS. CORN USED IN THIS PRODUCT MAY CONTAIN TRACES OF SOYBEANS.

BREAKFAST
RECIPES

Grandma Beryl's Waffles and Pancakes

2 Cups Bisquick (make sure to read package and make sure it is safe for you.)

1/3 cup oil

1 1/3 cups club soda

Replacement for 1 egg, 1 ½ tsp egg replacer powder and 2 tbsp warm water (whisk together powder and water until frothy)

Mix Bisquick, oil and egg mixture together, fold in club soda.

This mixture makes pancakes and waffles.

Cook and enjoy. They are crispy on the outside and soft and fluffy on the inside. A little bite of heaven in the morning.

French Toast Sticks

1 cup dairy free milk

2 ½ tsp flour

1 ½ tsp sugar

½ tsp vanilla extract

Dash of salt

Cinnamon sugar mixture (1/4 c sugar and ¼ tsp cinnamon mixed together)

Slices of bread cut in strips

Whisk together milk, flour, sugar, salt, and vanilla.

Pour mixture into a shallow dish

Slice bread into strips

Heat dairy free margarine in a skillet over medium heat.

Lightly dredge bread slices through wet mixture. Make sure not to let soak in mixture or it will stay soggy even after being cooked. You can use any type of store bought frozen bread if you want, but I never have it on hand so I just use regular bread.

Sprinkle with cinnamon sugar and place on griddle.

Cook until golden brown.

Donut Love

This recipe was so amazing to find. I am so heartbroken every time my son asks for a donut and I have to say no.

This recipe is simple and very versatile.

One thing I would absolutely recommend is getting a donut pan. They are very inexpensive and so worth telling your allergy person that YES you can have a delicious donut.

¾ cup dairy free milk + 1 tbsp apple cider vinegar= buttermilk

2 ¾ cup allergy friendly cake mix powder

2 tbsp melted dairy free margarine

½ cup applesauce

Preheat oven to 425°

Spray a donut pan with nonstick cooking spray

Whisk together ¾ cup dairy free milk and add 1 tbsp apple cider vinegar. Set it aside and let it sit for about 5 minutes and it will make buttermilk.

Place all ingredients into a bowl and mix with a hand mixer for 30 seconds. Fill donut pan with batter about 2/3 of the way full. I actually find it is easiest to put the batter into a large ziplock bag, cut the tip and fill the donut pan.

Bake for 7 to 9 minutes or until a toothpick comes out clean.

Glaze or decorate any way you wish. These are really moist and delicious.

Donut Holes

Make batter the same as Donut Love, page 25

You can also add any flavoring to the batter, such as lemon extract, grenadine, orange extract, cocoa powder or just add some dairy free chocolate chips.

Preheat oven to 425°F

For this recipe I like to use my cake pop pan

Coat the pan with non-stick cooking spray

Bake for 7 to 9 minutes

Spoon batter into the cake pop holes

Remove from oven and cool

You can "dress" these anyway you like:

Shake them in a cinnamon sugar mixture

Donut Glaze

¼ cup dairy free milk

2 cups powdered sugar

1 tsp vanilla

Place all ingredients into a saucepan over medium heat and whisk to combine. Heat for about 5 minutes. Dunk or pour over donuts.

Orange Rolls

1 package crescent rolls (there is a pretty wide selection of allergy friendly crescent rolls, either name brand or store brand. Just make sure to read the label to make sure they are safe for you)

Filling:

3 tbsp melted dairy free margarine

½ cup sugar

Zest of one orange

Icing:

1 cup powdered sugar

1-3 tbsp dairy free creamer (you can find it where you buy your dairy free milk)

1 dash salt

1 tsp orange extract

Preheat oven to 375°

For the icing mix all ingredients together and set aside.

Roll out crescent rolls and mend the lines with your fingers to make a long sheet.

Mix the filling ingredients together and spread across the crescent roll sheet.

Roll the dough and slice into 6 large or 12 small rolls.

Place into a greased round cake pan and bake for 12-15 minutes or until tops begin to brown.

Remove from oven and frost rolls while warm.

Enjoy.

*** You can also make Lemon rolls like this by subbing out the orange zest and extract for lemon flavoring and zest. A different, but delicious roll.

Cinnamon Rolls

1 tube of crescent rolls (find allergy friendly ones, there is a pretty good selection of them, brand name or store brand)

Filling:

2 tbsp softened dairy free margarine

½ cup brown sugar

2 tsp cinnamon

Icing:

1 cup powdered sugar

1-3 tbsp dairy free creamer (you can find it where you buy the dairy free milk)

1 dash salt

1 tsp vanilla extract

Preheat oven to 375°

Roll out the crescent rolls and mend the lines with your fingers to make a long sheet.

Mix the ingredients for the filling by stirring together the cinnamon and brown sugar, then fork in the softened dairy free margarine and spread across the crescent roll sheet.

Roll the dough up into a log and slice into 6 large rolls or 10 medium sized rolls. Place rolls into a greased round cake pan and bake for 12 to 15 minutes or until golden brown.

While rolls are baking mix ingredients for icing and set aside.

Remove rolls from oven and frost rolls while still warm, but not hot.

Banana Crumb Muffins

1 ½ cups all-purpose flour

1 tsp baking powder

1 tsp baking soda

½ tsp salt

3 bananas mashed

¾ cup white sugar

Replacement for 1 egg (1 ½ tsp egg replacer powder and 2 tbsp warm water) Use a wire whisk and whip until frothy

1/3 cup dairy free margarine, melted

1/3 cup packed brown sugar

2 tbsp all purpose flour

1/8 tsp cinnamon

1 tbsp dairy free margarine

Heat oven to 375°.

Prepare muffin tins with papers.

Combine flour, salt, baking soda, and baking powder.

In a separate bowl, combine the wet ingredients. Mix the bananas, melted dairy free margarine, sugar and egg replacement mixture.

Add the wet mixture into the dry mixture just until moistened. Use an ice cream scoop to fill the muffin tins.

In a smaller bowl, combine the brown sugar, cinnamon and 2 tbsp flour. Fork in 1 tbsp dairy free margarine to make a crumb topping and crumb it up on the muffin tops.

Bake for 15 to 18 minutes. Make sure you check doneness with a toothpick.

Enjoy the way these muffins make your house smell.

Chocolate Chip Chewy Bars

2 cups rolled oats

1 cups crispy rice cereal

¼ cup dairy free margarine

½ cup brown sugar

¼ cup honey

2 tsp vanilla extract

½ cup mini chocolate chips

      Lay parchment paper in a 9x13 pan. Melt dairy free margarine over medium heat. To the saucepan add the honey, vanilla and brown sugar.

Now pour oats and cereal into a medium bowl and stir. Add liquid mixture to dry mixture and fold together to combine.

Smoosh across 9x13 pan. Smoosh chocolate chips into top of the bars with a square of wax paper.

*** sometimes I let the mixture cool a little and then add the chocolate chips and stir so they get all through the bar. Just make sure it cools a bit or else the chips will melt☹**Refrigerate for at least 1 hour. Remove from fridge and Enjoy. These are so tasty. Try not to eat the whole pan.

Dairy Free Buttermilk

I have never been able to find a dairy free buttermilk in any stores. But I have found it is very easy to make at home.

1 tbsp lemon juice or

1 tbsp apple cider vinegar or

1 tbsp white vinegar

1 cup soy or allergy friendly milk of your choice

Measure out 1 tablespoon of the lemon juice, apple cider vinegar or white vinegar. All these work very well, it is really your choice.

Pour in 1 cup of soy or milk of your choice.

Stir and let sit for about 5-10 minutes and you have made buttermilk. It will begin to curdle the milk, which thickens it.

This makes 1 cup of liquid.

Use in any recipe that calls for dairy free buttermilk.

SOUPS

&

STEWS

Betty's Chili

1 lb ground turkey or beef

1 can kidney beans

1 can diced tomatoes

2 cans tomato soup

1 can water

1 package Chili seasoning mix of your choice, beware some contain milk.

Brown turkey over medium heat. Add Seasoning mix and stir into the meat.

Add beans, tomatoes, soup and water. Stir all ingredients and bring to a simmer. Turn the heat down to low and let it go for about 1 to 2 hours.

Top with tortilla chips and a side of crusty bread.

Chicken Noodle Soup

4 cups allergy friendly chicken broth

1 chopped carrot

1 stalk of celery, diced

Pepper to taste

1 cup of chicken, chopped into bite size pieces or shredded, whichever you prefer.

½ cup uncooked allergy friendly noodle of choice (I like penne or chopped up spaghetti)

Place broth, carrot, celery and pepper into a saucepan. Heat to a boil.

Once it is boiling, add the chicken and pasta to the pool and reduce the heat to medium. Cook until pasta is done to your liking.

Sometimes I like to cook the noodle in a separate pot and add to the individual bowls and ladle the broth mixture over the noodles in the bowl.

Brown Beef Stew

1/3 cup flour

¼ tsp pepper

½ tsp celery salt

2 lbs stew beef, trimmed and cut into bite sized pieces

¼ cup oil, vegetable or canola

¼ cup chopped onion

1 clove minced onion

4 cups hot water

4 beef bouillon cubes or 4 tsp beef bouillon powder, make sure it is allergy friendly

½ tsp Worcestershire sauce

Dissolve the bouillon cubes or beef powder in hot water to make beef water.

On a large piece of wax paper place: flour, pepper and celery salt. Mix well and drip meat pieces in until well coated. Save flour.

Heat oil in a deep pot and slowly brown meat a few pieces at a time.

**Don't crowd the meat; it will steam instead of browning.

Remove pieces as they brown. Repeat until all meat is brown. Remove all meat.

Add onion and garlic to empty pan to brown a little.

Add some beef water so it won't burn, just enough to cover and cook for a few minutes until tender.

Add all the rest of the 4 cups of liquid and meat. Add ½ tsp Worcestershire sauce.

Now place 1 cup of cold water in measuring cup and add remaining flour. Whisk until smooth and add to the pan.

Cover and bring to a boil and turn down to very low temp with vent on cover open and top ajar. Cook a good 3 hours.

Add carrots first because they take longer to cook, then add potatoes and cook until tender.

Serve and enjoy.

SIDE DISHES

Homemade Croutons

6 slices of slightly stale allergy friendly bread

Olive Oil

Salt and Pepper

Garlic Powder

Preheat oven to 375°

Cut bread into bite size cubes

In a large bowl place bread cubes, drizzle with olive oil, salt and pepper to taste and sprinkle with garlic powder.

Stir all ingredients together making sure all bread cubes are covered with the olive oil.

Pour bread cubes out onto a cookie sheet and bake for 15 minutes or until lightly browned. Or if you like them extra crunchy cook them a little longer.

Party Rice

1 small green pepper, diced

1 small onion, shopped

10 oz frozen corn, thawed

1 cup chicken broth

1 tbsp oil

1 cup mild salsa (please read label to make sure it is allergy friendly)

1 ½ cup white rice

Heat oil in large skillet over medium heat. Place pepper and onion in pan and cook until tender.

Stir in the chicken broth, corn and salsa. Bring up to a boil.

Stir in rice and cover. Pull pan away from the heat and let it sit for 5 minutes.

Fluff with fork and enjoy.

Great to take for a dish to pass.

Taco Salad

1 LB ground beef

1 package taco seasoning (your allergy friendly choice)

1 head of iceberg lettuce, chopped

1 large tomato, diced

¾ cup dairy and egg free mayonnaise (found in organic section at market)

1 small bottle of taco sauce

2 cups shredded dairy free cheddar cheese (optional)

1 bag of corn chips (make sure you read the package to ensure they are allergy friendly)

To make the dressing, stir together the dairy and egg free mayo and the taco sauce, set aside.

Cook the ground beef on medium heat until no longer pink, add taco seasoning packet and cook according to packet's directions. Let cool.

In a large bowl, combine lettuce, tomato, taco beef, cheese if desired, and dressing. Slightly crush corn chips and add to the bowl.

Stir everybody together and serve immediately. This salad is a real crowd pleaser.

Also if you are not serving this immediately, you can add all things together except the dressing. Dress this salad at the last minute.

Taco Dip

8 oz dairy free cream cheese, softened

8 oz dairy free sour cream

1 packet of taco seasoning, make sure to read and that it is allergy friendly

Shredded lettuce

1 tomato, diced

4 green onions, chopped

1 cup dairy free cheddar cheese, shredded

Blend dairy free cream cheese and dairy free sour cream together with a hand mixer until smooth.

Stir in taco seasoning packet until well combined. Spread into a pie plate.

Top with lettuce, tomato, green onions and dairy free cheddar cheese.

Pop into the fridge to chill until ready to serve. I usually let it refrigerate for at least 1 hour.

Enjoy the compliments on this dip. It is really yummy and addictive

Grandma's Potato Salad

5lb bag of red potatoes

2 stalks of celery, peeled

½ a red onion

1 tbsp sugar

1 squirt of yellow mustard

Allergy friendly mayonnaise—about 1 cup

Salt and Pepper to taste

Paprika

Place potatoes in a large pot, fill with water and boil. Simmer until potatoes are fork tender. Potatoes should be tender, but not overcooked.

Drain in strainer and let cool for about 15 minutes. Peel potatoes when slightly warm. Chop into bite size pieces. Chop celery and onion and stir into potatoes.

Add sugar, mustard and allergy free mayo. Season with salt and pepper and feel free to add more salt and pepper and mayo to taste. Make sure you stir all ingredients together while potatoes are still warm. Garnish with paprika , chill in fridge for at least 1 hour and enjoy.

Roasted Carrots

5 lb bag of carrots, peeled and cut- or as many as you will eat

Drizzle of olive oil

Salt and pepper to taste

**This recipe works with all kinds of vegetables.

Preheat oven to 425°

Peel and cut carrots according to your liking. They can be sliced, chopped, julienned, whatever your heart desires.

Also you can use any vegetable you like; sometimes I use asparagus or zucchini and summer squash.

Arrange veggies on cookie sheet.

Drizzle with olive oil and mix around to coat all veggies.

Sprinkle with salt and pepper.

Bake for 20 minutes or until tender.

Super Tasty Asparagus

1 lb asparagus

2 tbsp dairy free margarine

2 tbsp water

Salt and pepper to taste

Chop asparagus into 1 inch pieces

Heat dairy free margarine in a medium skillet over medium heat. Add asparagus and water, but leave the tips out for now. Cook for about 5-8 minutes or until fork tender. Toss the tops into the pan and cook for 2 minutes. Add salt and pepper to taste. Serve and enjoy.

Sweet Potato Casserole

2 large cans of yams

1 cup brown sugar

½ cup of softened dairy free margarine

Preheat oven to 350°

Drain cans of yams and pour into a 2 qt casserole dish

In a medium bowl, mix together the brown sugar and softened dairy free margarine. Use a fork to mix together to make a crumb mixture.

Scatter over yams and make sure all are completely covered. You can double the crumb topping if you like to make a really thick crust.

Bake for 30 minutes or until golden brown and bubbly.

Homemade Bread Crumbs

6 slices of allergy friendly bread

Preheat oven to 375°

Layer bread slices onto cookie sheet and place in oven to get toasty, about 6-8 minutes.

Remove from oven and place into food processor to pulse them into breadcrumbs.

This will make about 1 cup of breadcrumbs.

If you want to make seasoned breadcrumbs, add salt and pepper to taste and about 1 tbsp of Italian seasoning.

Use these in any recipe that calls for breadcrumbs.

MAIN DISHES

Eggless "Egg" Roll Wrappers

This is a wonderful allergy friendly recipe and is so versatile. Enjoy.

2 cups all purpose flour

½ tsp salt

½ cup warm water

Cornstarch

To begin place the flour and salt into a bowl and sift it until it is thoroughly combined.

Take the warm water and add a little at a time. You need to stir it to combine so take it slow. This will make the dough very firm.

Pour some flour on a board and begin to knead the dough until it becomes smooth.

This takes about 15 minutes. Then cover it with a towel and let it be for about 20 minutes all by itself.

Now take about half the dough and roll it out a bit. I usually roll it through my hand cranked pasta maker until it's very thin, but you can use a rolling pin if you like. Keep rolling until all dough is used.

Then you can cut them to whatever shape you please, egg roll shape, wonton shape, spring roll shape, etc.

Then if you need to store them just put them in a freezer bag with a little bit of cornstarch and place in the freezer or fridge

Taco Rolls

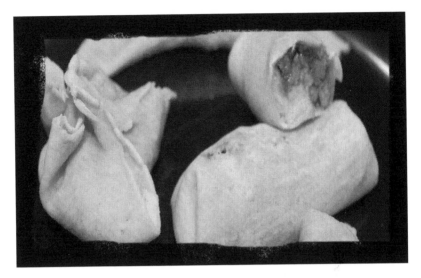

Eggless Egg roll wrappers, recipe page 62

1 lb ground chicken (you can use beef or turkey if you like)

1 package taco seasoning (allergy friendly version of course)

½ tsp garlic powder

1 medium onion, chopped

1 cup dairy free sour cream

Taco sauce for dipping

Preheat oven to 375°

Brown ground chicken and onion in a skillet over medium heat until fully cooked.

Add taco seasoning and ½ cup water

Simmer until water is absorbed, about 10 minutes.

Stir in dairy free sour cream until combined.

Let cool completely

Dip each eggless roll wrapper in water.

Place about 2 tbsp of meat in each wrapper and roll up. Roll according to the shape you desire.

Brush with water and bake at 375° for 20 minutes or until brown.

These are so tasty.

Handmade Pasta

1 cup all purpose flour

1 cup semolina flour

1 Tbsp olive oil

1/3 cup water

Dash of salt

Sift together the semolina and all-purpose flour

Sift onto clean work surface (cupboard or wooden board)

Add dash of salt and make a well in the middle of the flour.

Pour olive oil in the well and add water a few tablespoons at a time until you like the consistency.

Knead the mixture all together and get it mixed all up.

You will need to add a little more ap flour a little at a time in order to keep it from sticking. Dough is finished when it's not sticky anymore.

Let it sit for about 30 minutes. Place on a floured board and roll out.

You can make any shape pasta with this dough, either with a pasta machine or by hand.

To make spaghetti or fettuccine, roll the dough out to desired thickness and cut strips with a knife to desired width.

Cook and enjoy.

Pasta Broccoli

1lb of handmade pasta, recipe on page 66 or allergy friendly pasta of your choice

4 or 5 cloves of minced garlic

4 tbsp olive oil

Salt and pepper to taste

2 cups broccoli florets

Red pepper flakes, optional

First steam the broccoli however you wish, on the stove or in the microwave (cover with water and cook for 90 seconds)

Cook and drain pasta according to directions on package.

In a large frying pan, heat the olive oil, garlic and salt and pepper for a couple of minutes until the oil heats up. Add the broccoli and cook for about 5 minutes.

Place drained pasta in a large bowl, add the broccoli and garlic sauce.

Toss all together, add more olive oil if necessary, season with salt and pepper and add the red pepper flakes if you like a little spice.

Serve and enjoy.

Goulash

1 lb ground beef

15 oz can of tomato sauce

2 cloves minced garlic

Salt and pepper to taste

1 can diced tomatoes

1 can crushed tomatoes

1 medium green pepper, diced

1 bay leaf

1 lb allergy friendly pasta of your choice, I usually use elbow noodles

In a large pan brown the ground beef and drain off excess grease when cooked. Add tomato sauce, garlic, diced and crushed tomatoes, green pepper, bay leaf and salt and pepper. Stir all ingredients together and let simmer for about 30 minutes.

In a separate pot, fill with water and bring to a boil. Add pasta and cook according to the directions on the pasta box. Drain and add to the beef mixture.

Stir to combine and remove bay leaf.

Chicken Marsala

4 chicken breasts, boneless

4 tbsp dairy-free margarine

½ cup flour

4 tbsp oil

Salt and pepper to taste

1 cup marsala wine

2 cups fresh or canned mushrooms, sliced

Wash chicken and slice into thin strips

In a medium bowl, stir together flour, salt and pepper.

Place chicken into bowl and cover with mixture

Heat oil and margarine in pan

Cook the chicken until both sides have a nice brown crust. I turn them a few times to make sure all of the chicken gets nice and almost crispy. Put the mushrooms in and cook for a few more minutes to get the flavors together.

Pour the Marsala wine into the pan and cover the chicken pieces.

Turn chicken over a couple of times and reposition the pieces to make sure the wine and chicken are all mixed and chicken is covered.

Place lid on pan and simmer for about 15 to 20 minutes or until the sauce is at your desired thickness. I turn chicken after about 10 minutes and stir wine.

Enjoy this simple and delicious meal.

Mustard Fried Chicken

1 lb of chicken sliced into tenders

½ cup of Dijon mustard (make sure it is allergy friendly)

Salt and pepper to taste

1 cup of panko bread crumbs (make sure they are allergy friendly)

4 tbsp vegetable or canola oil

2 tbsp dairy free margarine

Sauce:

1 tbsp dairy free margarine

1 tbsp flour

½ cup dairy free creamer

1 tbsp Dijon mustard

Season chicken with salt and pepper.

Pour Dijon mustard into a medium bowl, and pour panko crumbs onto a plate.

Dredge chicken through mustard and into panko. Cover chicken completely and shake off excess. Lay on a plate to rest. Continue with the remaining chicken pieces and let them sit. I don't know why, but this step really makes a difference in how the chicken tastes at the end. So make sure to let the chicken sit for about 10 minutes.

Meanwhile heat the oil and dairy free margarine in a large skillet.

Place chicken pieces into pan and cook until golden brown on all sides. You may have to do this in batches because you should not crowd the chicken while it cooks.

In a small saucepan heat dairy free margarine and flour. Whisk for about a minute to cook out the flour taste. Whisk in the dairy free creamer and mustard. Cook until it gets a little thick, or until your desired consistency. Season with salt and pepper.

Pour over chicken and serve.

With this recipe the sauce is optional; it is fantastic with or without the sauce.

Enjoy.

Mini Chicken Pot Pies

1 can allergy friendly refrigerated biscuits, jumbo works best

¼ cup melted dairy free margarine

3 tbsp flour

1 cup chicken broth

¼ to ½ cup soy or coconut milk creamer, found next to soy milk at store

Salt and pepper to taste

2 cups diced or shredded cooked chicken

1 cup frozen peas, thawed

Whisk melted dairy free margarine and flour over low heat and let it cook for a couple minutes, whisking consistently.

Stir in chicken broth and ¼ cup soy creamer. (Start with less and add as you go, you need less soy creamer to make things thicken. If you add too much it will never thicken).

Cook, stirring constantly until sauce is thick.

Add 1 tsp salt, 2 cups cooked chicken and thawed vegetables.

In a muffin pan, press 1 biscuit in each opening, spoon mixture into the biscuit. Fill about ¾ full. Pinch dough together at tops and sprinkle with salt and pepper. There will be some sauce left over to serve on top of pies before serving.

Bake at 375° for 20-22 min or until biscuits are golden brown.

Ladel with remaining sauce if desired.

Serve and enjoy.

Thai "Peanut Free" Chicken

Marinade for chicken:

1 pound of chicken sliced into tenders

½ cup soy sauce

1 tsp lemon juice

4 cloves of minced garlic

2 tbsp sugar

2 tbsp sesame oil

Whisk all ingredients together. Place chicken in a large ziplock bag and pour marinade over chicken. Close bag and smoosh marinade all over chicken. Throw in the fridge for at least 1 hour.

"Peanut free" Sauce:

2 cloves of minced garlic

2 tbsp soy sauce

¼ cup rice wine vinegar

1 tbsp brown sugar

½ cup peanut free spread of your choice. We like the sunflower spread

Dash of red pepper flakes for some heat

Whisk all these ingredients together until smooth. You can do this by hand or in a blender.

Grill the chicken until cooked thoroughly and remove from heat when done.

Serve with the sauce for dipping!

Enjoy!

Turkey in the Crock Pot

1 frozen turkey breast (6-6 ½ lbs)

2 tsp vegetable oil

Salt and pepper

1 medium onion

4 garlic cloves

Pull turkey out of freezer and let it sit, in order to get the packaging off, but turkey will still be frozen when placed in Crockpot.

Smoosh oil all over turkey and sprinkle with salt and pepper.

Lay turkey breast in crock pot with the boney side down.

Chop onion and garlic into large chunks and position around turkey

Put cover on Crockpot and cook on low for 6 to 8 hours.

MMMMMM Thanksgiving in a pot.

BBQ Chicken Legs

Chicken Legs (Use as many as you will eat)

BBQ sauce of your choice

*Place wire cooling rack on foil lined cookie sheet

*Put chicken on rack and brush with BBQ sauce

Bake at 350° for 3 hours, turning and basting chicken every 30 minutes.

Chicken legs will bake to this delicious crispy, amazingness of BBQ goodness.

Casserole Pizza

3 cups of Bisquick baking mix (make sure it is allergy friendly for you)

¾ cup cold water

2 cloves crushed garlic

1 pound ground beef

½ tsp salt

1 can tomato sauce (15 oz)

½ cup chopped onion

1 tsp Italian seasoning

pepper to taste

½ cup chopped green pepper

1 small jar of sliced mushrooms, drained

1/2 cup chopped banana peppers

8oz shredded dairy free mozzarella cheese (optional)

Preheat oven to 425°

Spray 9x13 pan with nonstick cooking spray.

In a skillet, brown the ground beef, onion, garlic, salt and pepper.

Then stir in the tomato sauce and Italian seasoning. Set aside.

In a medium bowl stir together the baking mix and water and mix until completely combined.

Roll dough out onto a floured board. Knead until dough is smooth and spreadable.

Place dough into 9x13 pan and spread out so it covers the whole pan and up the sides about ¾ in.

Pour meat mixture over dough and spread evenly. Top with mushrooms and peppers. Top with cheese if you like. I actually like it better without the cheese

Bake for about 20 minutes until pizza is heated through and crust is golden brown.

This pizza is fantastic.

Chicken Wing Pizza

9in pizza crust of your allergy friendly choice

2 cups of shredded cooked chicken

½ cups Frank's red hot sauce

2 tbsp melted dairy free margarine

Salt and pepper to taste

Dash of onion powder

Drizzle of olive oil

1 cup of shredded dairy free mozzarella cheese

In a medium bowl place cooked shredded chicken, season with salt and pepper and onion powder.

Melt dairy free margarine and stir in hot sauce. This is to taste, if you like it spicier add more hot sauce and less dairy free margarine. Pour over chicken and spices and place in fridge to marinate.

Drizzle olive oil on pizza dough, layer a small amount of dairy free cheese.

Spread chicken all over pizza dough. Sprinkle remaining cheese over chicken.

Bake according to dough directions.

Remove from oven and cool for 5 minutes.

Slice and enjoy.

Brown Sugar Glaze for Ham

1 cup brown sugar

2 Tbsp flour

½ tsp dried or prepared mustard

1/8 tsp cinnamon

3 Tbsp vinegar

3 Tbsp water

Place all ingredients into a medium sized bowl and stir together.

Spread on top of ham before baking.

Candied Polish Sausage

4 links of polska kielbaska (most are milk-free, but make sure you read the label!!)

2 cans of beer

2 cups of brown sugar

Cut sausage links into slices about ½ in thick

Place into bottom of Crockpot

Pour beer over sausage until sausage is just covered by the liquid

Stir in brown sugar.

Cook on low for 6 to 8 hours and enjoy.

Believe me everyone will be asking for the recipe.

RIBS!!!

My boys LOVE ribs!! And these do not disappoint!!

For the Sauce

1 cup Ketchup

2 tbsp mustard

½ cup brown sugar

2 tbsp apple cider vinegar

2 tbsp honey

1 small onion, finely chopped

2 tbsp Worcestershire sauce

Add all ingredients into frying pan and heat on medium until the onion is cooked.

Take ribs of your choice, pork or beef, and place on grill. Grill both sides of ribs to get a nice crust on!!

Remove from grill and place into crock pot. Pour barbecue sauce over ribs and cook on low for 6-8 hours. Oh my goodness you will absolutely Love these. They stay juicy and don't get dried out.

Meatloaf

2 lbs of meatloaf mix (it is a mix of ground beef, pork and veal.) I f that isn't available you can use all ground beef

1 cup homemade bread crumbs, Page 43

¾ cup water

1/3 cup ketchup

1 medium onion, grated

Egg replacer + water to replace 2 eggs

Preheat oven to 350°

Measure out all ingredients into a large bowl and stir to combine. I usually use my hands to mix.

Place into a 13x9 in pan and shape into a loaf. Take about ½ cup of ketchup and spread over the top .

Bake for about 90 minutes or until edges are crispy.

Let the meatloaf rest for about 10 minutes before slicing.

Enjoy!!

Meatballs

½ lb beef

3 tbsp water

½ lb Italian sausage

2 tbsp veg or canola oil

1 small onion, grated

1 ½ tsp Worcestershire sauce

1 tbsp parsley

1 clove garlic, minced

1 tsp salt

1 tsp Italian seasoning

½ tsp pepper

Egg replacer for 1 egg, follow directions on box

1 cup panko crumbs, make sure they are allergy friendly or you can always make your own bread crumbs!

1 tsp red pepper flakes, optional. It depends on how much zip you want. The sausage will already add a little spice, but if you like zip you should add it in!!

Preheat oven to 400°

In a large bowl combine all ingredients. Shape into balls of your desired size. Place onto a cookie sheet.

Bake for 20-25 minutes.

Enjoy!!! These are really tasty! You can serve these alone as an appetizer or on a heaping plate of pasta and sauce!! Whichever way you choose is delicious.

SNACKS

Microwave Popcorn

If you are an allergy parent then you understand what an obstacle finding microwavable popcorn can be. Well here is the answer to your prayers.

½ cup popcorn kernels

Brown paper bag

Add popcorn kernels to paper bag

Fold bag over twice so it is definitely closed

Stick bag into microwave and cook for 2- 3 minutes or until popcorn stops popping. If the popping starts to slow down before 3 minutes then pull it out so it doesn't burn.

Sprinkle with salt or melted dairy free margarine.

Enjoy.

Caramel Corn

1 Cup popcorn kernels

2 cups brown sugar

½ cup light corn syrup

1 tsp salt

1 stick dairy free margarine

½ tsp baking soda

1 tsp vanilla

Pop your popcorn how you like, air popper or pour the kernels into a brown paper bag and pop in microwave for 2 minutes and pull out when popping slows down! Popping depends on the strength of your microwave.

Then in a saucepan, place the brown sugar, corn syrup, salt and dairy free margarine. Turn it to high heat and bring to a boil. Once it is boiling bring the heat down and let it bubble for 5 min. You really don't need to stir it much, just let it bubble away.

Take it off the heat and then put in the vanilla and baking soda. Empty the full saucepan over the popcorn into a roasting pan and stir all together. Bake for 1 hour mixing it up every 15 min.

Cool and get ready to Cracker Jack.

Strawberry Salsa with Dippin' Strips

1 pint of strawberries

1 apple, finely chopped

2 tsp lime juice

Fresh mint

1 tbsp sugar

Chop strawberries after removing stems. Adjust size of chop according to your liking.

Mix with remaining ingredients and place into refrigerator for at least 2 hours.

This will let the sugar break the strawberries down and it makes the delightful sweetness come out in the salsa.

Dippin' Strips

Slice flour tortillas into triangles

Spray with cooking spray

Sprinkle with cinnamon sugar

Bake at 375° until crispy, about 4-5 min

Dip away. Yummy.

Easy Milkshake

This is a very simple and delicious milkshake recipe that you can completely make your own!!

1 cup non-dairy ice cream (the flavor of your choice)

½ cup to ¾ cup soy creamer-make sure it its allergy friendly for you. I like to use the creamer better than milk because it makes the milkshake thicker and creamier, but soy or coconut milk works too.

Place non-dairy ice cream into blender and add creamer. Blend until desired thickness or thinness and enjoy.

Feel free to add whatever additions you wish. Allergy friendly sprinkles, non-dairy whipped cream, cherries, strawberries, or allergy friendly sandwich cookies broken up.

Smoothies

You can make this smoothie with any combination of frozen fruit, juice and dairy free yogurt.

1 cup of frozen fruit, (pineapple, strawberry, raspberries, etc)

1 banana

½ cup of soy or coconut milk yogurt, I like to use plain or vanilla

Add all ingredients to a blender and pulse until smooth.

Enjoy!.

DESSERTS

Easy Peasy Cake

This cake's secret lies in what you do after it's baked. The step of putting it in the freezer makes it taste like it came from a bakery.

1 boxed cake mix

(There are a couple name brand ones that don't have any egg, dairy, peanut or tree nut) The flavors I use are Classic Yellow, Devil's Food or Lemon Supreme

Mix cake according to directions with water, oil and egg replacer.

Substitute egg replacer for egg. (When mixing egg replacer with water, make sure you mix it with the hand mixer or really whip it with a wire whisk. That ensures the mixture gets very frothy and will give you the best results).

Bake according to directions on box.

Under bake the cake. For example if it calls to bake it for 27 minutes, start checking at 22 minutes. Check with a toothpick and bake it till it's not goopy. There will be cake on the toothpick.

Cool slightly, approximately 5 minutes. Place wax paper over cake and then tin foil. Place in freezer for about 60 minutes. Then move it to the refrigerator and leave there until ready to serve. Quickly frost before serving.

Keep chilled in refrigerator after serving.

This is so tasty and easy! People will never believe it is allergy friendly.

Homemade Frosting

1 cup shortening or dairy free margarine

1 tsp vanilla

1 lb powdered sugar

4 tbsp dairy free milk

Mix shortening and powdered sugar with a hand mixer until creamy. It will take a few minutes.

Don't get nervous because the consistency looks terrible, it will come together. All of a sudden it will look like frosting☺

At that point, add the vanilla and mix together. Add milk in last and do it 1 tbsp at a time to desired consistency.

Homemade Sprinkles

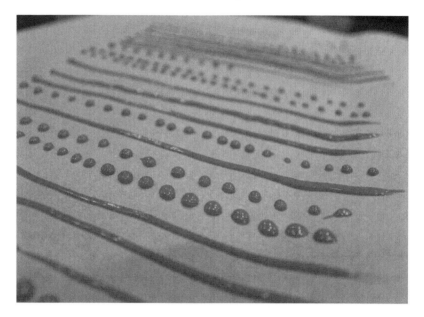

Every kid loves sprinkles and good luck finding allergy friendly ones! They are all processed in a factory with peanuts and tree nuts. So here are great homemade ones you can feel safe about.

To make the sprinkles:

1 cup powdered sugar

1-3 tbsp dairy free milk

1 tbsp light corn syrup

Food coloring of choice (1-2 drops per cup of powdered sugar)

Mix all ingredients together with a hand mixer. Start with 1 tbsp of dairy free milk and add to desired consistency. The thicker the consistency the better.

Next place the mixture into a baggie and cut across the corner to make a small tip so your dots or lines are thin.

Lay out a piece of parchment paper onto a cookie sheet.

Squeeze out sprinkle batter either in thin lines or dots depending on how big you want your sprinkles.

Let them sit out for a few hours or overnight to dry out a bit.

If you made lines, chop them up into desired size for your sprinkles.

Quick Pudding

1 package pudding and pie filling packet, almost all brands are allergy friendly, just find one that works for you

1 to 1 ½ cup dairy free milk

*** The secret to making quick allergy friendly pudding is to add less milk than it actually calls for. For instance if the package calls for 2 cups of milk, add 1 to 1 ½ cups of dairy free milk. If you add too much milk it will never set. Just the right amount of dairy free milk will make fantastic quick pudding.

Pour the packet into a medium bowl and add the cold dairy free milk.

Whisk together for 2 minutes and let set in fridge for about 20-30 minutes!

You can use this pudding for pies or frozen treats.

Yogurt Pops

2 containers of dairy free yogurt, the flavor of your choice

Popsicle holders

Pour dairy free yogurt into empty popsicle holders and fill to the top.

Place in freezer and allow at least 4 hours to completely freeze.

Enjoy.

These are a nice treat and they freeze beautifully.

***This also works with allergy friendly pudding, found on page 105 to make pudding pops.

Banana Pudding Pie

1 ¼ cups allergy friendly graham cracker crumbs

¼ cup sugar

4 tbsp dairy free margarine, melted

1 large package of allergy friendly banana instant pudding and pie filling packet or 2 small packages

1 ¾ cups of cold soy or coconut milk***

1 banana, sliced

Preheat oven 350°

Mix graham cracker crumbs, sugar and butter in a bowl

Press crumb mixture into bottom and up side of 9 inch pie plate

Bake for 6 to 8 minutes

In a medium bowl whisk the soy or coconut milk into the pudding powder and beat for 2 minutes.

Slice the banana and layer it in the bottom of the cooled crust.

Pour pudding into crust.

Top with dairy free whipped cream, recipe on page 109

Let set for 1 hour or more in the fridge.

***Package will call for more milk, but when using dairy free milk you have to use less or it will never set.

Pictured top: Cooled crust with layered bananas

Pictured bottom: Banana Pudding Pie

__Dairy Free Whipped Cream__

1 can full fat coconut milk, chilled and drained

1/3 cup powdered sugar

1 tsp vanilla

Whip coconut milk until fluffy, it will take a little bit, about 5 minutes. Whip in powdered sugar until stiff peaks appear.

Serve cold and enjoy.

Pictured: Strawberry shortpies

With Dairy Free Whipped Cream

Strawberry Shortpies

1 refrigerated allergy friendly pie crust

1 quart fresh strawberries

½ cup sugar

Preheat oven to 350°

Slice tops off strawberries and cut up in a bowl.

Mash slightly and sprinkle generously with sugar. Refrigerate for at least 4 hours.

Roll out refrigerated pie crust and cut into circles. I use a circle cookie cutter. Make sure you cut the circles big enough to fit in the muffin tins.

Place each circle into muffin tin openings and poke fork holes in bottoms

Bake according to directions on pie crust box.

Let cool.

Fill mini pies with strawberries and top with dairy free whipped cream. (see page 109 for dairy free whipped cream recipe)

Enjoy.

Strawberry Pretzel Salad

Crust:

2 cups of crushed allergy friendly pretzels

1 stick of melted dairy free margarine

3 tbsp of sugar

Preheat oven to 400°

Stir together the pretzels, sugar and melted dairy free margarine and spread into a 9 x 13 pan. Bake for 8 minutes and set aside to let cool.

Cool Layer:

8 oz of softened dairy free cream cheese

1 cup of dairy free whipped cream, recipe on page 109

1 cup sugar

Blend all ingredients together with a hand mixer until smooth. Spread onto the cooled crust.

Finishing Layer:

2 cups of boiling water

2 small packages of strawberry gelatin (make sure it's allergy friendly)

2 10oz packages of frozen strawberries

Stir the water and gelatin packages together until the gelatin is dissolved. Add the frozen strawberries into the mix. You need the strawberries to still be frozen in order for the gelatin to quick set. Pour this mixture onto the cool layer and refrigerate for 2 hours.

Enjoy! This is really delicious.

I know this looks like a sloppy mess and it is, but OH MY, it is soooo delicious. It is creamy and salty and crunchy and sweet!! You absolutely have to try this!! P.S. it is best when eaten the same day as it's made. Enjoy.

"Peanut Butter" Balls

2 cups powdered sugar

4 cups crispy rice cereal (make sure it's allergy friendly)

2 cups peanut free spread, whichever one you use that is peanut free and allergy friendly

1 stick softened dairy free margarine

2 cups dairy free chocolate chips

Melt dairy free chocolate chips either over a double boiler or in microwave

Blend dairy free margarine and peanut free spread

Add powdered sugar, blend together

Stir in crispy rice cereal

Roll into balls, dip in melted chocolate

Refrigerate and enjoy. Yummy.

"Peanut Butter" Cups

2 cups peanut free spread of your choice

2 cups powdered sugar

1 stick softened dairy free margarine

Melted dairy free chocolate

Blend softened dairy free margarine and peanut free spread with hand mixer until creamy.

Add powdered sugar and blend until smooth. Roll mixture into small balls.

Lay muffin cup liners out on cupboard.

Take a small amount of melted chocolate and pour into bottom of muffin cup liner and smooth out with a spoon. Lay a peanut free ball into center on top of chocolate.

Pour more chocolate on top of ball and smooth over the top so they look like a "peanut" butter cup. Place in fridge to set and enjoy!!!

Apple Deliciousness

4 cups sliced apples (about 6 or 7 apples peeled and sliced)

¼ cup orange juice

1 cup sugar

¾ cup flour

½ tsp cinnamon

¼ cup dairy free margarine

Spread a little margarine onto pie plate. (I like to use the wrapper of margarine package and smoosh it all around the pie plate.

Pour sliced apples into pie plate

Pour orange juice all over top of apples

In a small bowl, combine sugar, flour, cinnamon and a dash of salt

Mix cold margarine into the combo with a fork

Cover apples with mixture

Bake at 375° for 45 min or until apples are fork tender and topping is crisp.

Crispy Rice Pops

6 cups crisped rice cereal (allergy friendly brand)

3 tablespoons dairy free margarine, melted

1 bag, 10 oz, allergy friendly marshmallows, mini or regular

Popsicle sticks

Take a large pot and melt dairy free margarine on medium heat.

Add marshmallows and stir constantly until melted.

Remove from heat and add crisped rice cereal.

Stir until combined.

Place wax paper on cookie sheet and pour pan onto sheet.

Take a square of wax paper and spray with non-stick cooking spray, use square to smoosh mixture out onto cookie sheet to flatten.

Cut into desired size squares and place Popsicle stick into square to make a crispy rice pop!

If desired dip treats into melted dairy free chocolate and add homemade sprinkles.

If you are just going to make regular treats and not pops, make sure you line a pan with wax paper and cover with wax paper and then a cover on the pan. When using dairy free margarine, the treats tend to go stale much quicker; the wax paper helps to keep them fresh for a few days.

Logie Bread

2 cans (16.3 oz each) refrigerated biscuits—many brands are allergy friendly

½ cup sugar

1 tsp cinnamon

1 cup firmly packed brown sugar

¾ cup melted dairy free margarine

Preheat oven to 350°

Grease a Bundt pan with shortening or cooking spray.

In a medium bowl add together the white sugar and cinnamon.

Divide biscuits and roll them one by one into the sugar mixture.

Make sure they are coated and arrange in pan.

Stir brown sugar and butter, and then pour over biscuits in pan.

Bake for 28 to 32 minutes or until golden brown. Cool in the pan for 10 minutes.

Flip pan onto serving plate.

Pull apart and enjoy warm or room temp! Either is delightful.

Ice Cream Shell

1 package dairy free chocolate chips

2 Tbsp coconut oil, you can find it in the organic section of your grocery store

Melt chips and coconut oil in microwave until melted. Stir every 20 seconds until melty and smooth.

Pour over allergy friendly ice cream and it hardens like magic and what a treat for an allergy kid to have something cool to eat, because they can never have the real kind.

Ice Cream Cake Crunchies

About 20 sandwich cookies (please read package to make sure they are allergy safe for you)

About 1 cup of ice cream shell, see page 122

Start with 1 sleeve of cookies at a time

Place cookies in food processor or place in a bag and crush the bejesus out of them so they are finely crushed.

Add the liquid shell to bowl, stir and keep adding together until you reach desired consistency.

Stir them together and let sit aside! These are really yummy.

These can be used to make Dairy Free Ice cream cakes or toppings for Ice Cream cones.

For the cake:

Spread a layer of Dairy free ice cream in a pan, schmear a thin layer of crunchies over cream and then top with another layer of dairy free ice cream. Then you can decorate however you like, with sprinkles or writing or dairy free whipped cream! Whatever floats your boat. Enjoy.

Fruit Dip

This dip is so creamy and tasty; it can be used to dip any kind of fruit! This is a definite kid favorite! The marshmallow part takes a little bit, but it's so worth it!

1 Tbsp gelatin

¼ cup cool water

1 cup sugar

1/3 cups water

1 tbsp honey

¼ tsp vanilla

Take a large mixing bowl and add ¼ cup water to 1 tbsp gelatin. Mix it together until it's well combined. Let it sit aside.

In a saucepan add the sugar, water, honey and vanilla. Boil those ingredients until they are rolling in the pan and gets this soft almost fluffy texture which is called soft ball stage or measures 238-240°F This only takes a couple of minutes on high.

Pour hot liquid into bowl with gelatin and mix on low with a hand or stand mixer until it is combined then gun it to high until sticky, about 10 minutes.

You should come out with awesome marshmallow fluff!! And allergy friendly to boot!! You can use this as a filling for cookie sandwiches or sunbutter and fluff sandwiches.

Now for the dip:

 2 cups homemade fluff

8 oz cream cheese

Take the fluff and 8oz of softened milk free cream cheese.

Mix with a hand or stand mixer to combine. Mix until smooth and creamy. Serve at room temp. If you do refrigerate this make sure you give it time to come back to room temp before serving.

This is really, really good.

Chocolate Chip Cookies

These are amazing! You could serve these at a party and no one would ever know they are allergy friendly!

2 ¼ cup flour

1 tsp baking soda

½ tsp salt

1 cup dairy free margarine, softened

½ cup sugar

1 cup brown sugar

1 tsp vanilla

Egg replacer for the equivalent of 2 eggs; follow directions on egg replacer box

1 small pkg of vanilla pudding mix (3.4oz), make sure it is allergy friendly for you

2 cups of dairy free chocolate chips

Preheat oven to 350°

Take a large bowl and cream together the softened dairy free margarine, sugar and brown sugar. Mix until creamy.

In a medium bowl stir together the flour, baking soda and salt. Set aside.

In a small bowl whip the egg replacer powder and warm water until frothy.

Add the egg replacer mixture and vanilla to the creamed margarine mixture and mix.

Next slowly incorporate the dry mixture to the wet until all is combined.

Then take the pudding packet and add to mixture and mix until smooth.

Fold in dairy free chocolate chips.

Line cookie sheet with parchment paper and spoon dough onto pan and bake for 8 to 10 minutes. Do not over bake.

**Sometimes I just use my hands to roll dough into balls onto the pans, then smoosh them down into cookie shapes. They won't spread out too much. The dough will appear a little dry, but don't worry they will come out awesome.

Chocolate Chip Cookie Cake

Take the Chocolate Chip Cookie, recipe, page 126

Preheat oven to 350°

Take a pizza stone or pizza pan and spread the cookie dough out on it.

Spread the dough almost to the edges, but leave a little room for it to expand, or make it as big as you want.

Bake fo 15 to 20 minutes. Make sure you don't overcook it!

Remove from oven and let cool.

Decorate it if you please.

Frozen Banana Bites

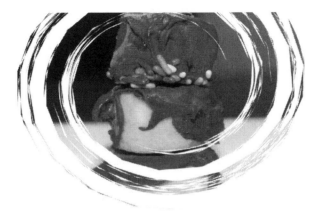

4 bananas, sliced and frozen

½ cup dairy free chocolate chips, melted

Slice bananas into ½in chunks, place into covered container and freeze for at least 2 hours.

Melt chocolate over double boiler or in microwave for 1 min, however you choose!

Dip frozen banana chunks into melted chocolate (it's just easier when the bananas are frozen so they don't fall apart and mush when dipping them into the melted chocolate).

Space them out onto wax paper, let the chocolate harden and then package to freeze. Let freeze for at least 2 hours.

Enjoy! Believe it or not, these taste pretty darn close to ice cream bites. Yummy.

I Can't Believe It's Not Peanut Butter Cookies

1 cup shortening

½ cup unsweetened applesauce

1 cup peanut free spread, I like the sunflower seed spread

1 tsp vanilla

1 Cup sugar

1 cup brown sugar

3 cups flour

2 tsp baking soda

Dash of salt

Preheat oven to 375°

In a large bowl cream the shortening, sugar and brown sugar together. Add the applesauce, peanut free spread, and vanilla. Mix until well combined.

In a medium bowl stir together the flour, baking soda and dash of salt.

Slowly incorporate the dry ingredients into the shortening mixture. Mix until all is combined and roll into balls. Place onto a parchment paper lined cookie sheet.

Take the balls and flatten them with a floured fork onto the cookie sheet.

Bake for 12 minutes. Enjoy.

Lemon Crinkle Cookies

1 box Lemon Flavored Cake Mix (allergy friendly one of course)

½ cup vegetable or canola oil

The equivalent of 2 eggs, you can use egg replacer powder and water

Preheat oven to 350°

In a medium bowl stir to combine the cake mix and oil.

In a small bowl, place egg replacer powder and warm water and whisk until very bubbly. This step is really important because whisking it up gives it the rising properties of a real egg!

Pour mixture into cake mix and stir just enough so that it's mixed.

Spoon cookies onto greased cookie sheet.

Bake for 10 minutes or until edges are golden brown.

Grandma Cosgrove's Cut-Out Cookies

1 cup softened dairy free margarine

2 cups sugar

¾ cup unsweetened applesauce

1 tsp cream of tartar (it is allergy safe even though it doesn't sound like it!)

1 ½ tsp baking soda, dissolved in 2 tbsp dairy free milk

1 tsp salt

1 tsp vanilla

4 ½ cups sifted flour

Confectioners or powdered sugar

In a large bowl cream dairy free margarine with sugar thoroughly. Add vanilla, dairy free milk with baking soda and applesauce. Mix until all is combined.

In a medium bowl stir together the flour, salt and cream of tartar. Slowly incorporate the wet mixture into the flour mixture until all is combined. Roll into a ball and chill for about an hour.

When ready to roll, remove dough from fridge and roll dough on board dusted with powdered sugar. I suggest pulling a small amount of dough out at a time and leaving the rest in the fridge. The allergy friendly dough needs to be cold to roll and to keep your sanity! Allergy friendly dough can get very sticky and gummy really quickly.

Cut cookies into desired shapes and bake on a parchment paper lined cookie sheet at 375° for 8-15 minutes. I know that sounds like a large window, but you don't want the edges to burn. So you definitely need to keep an eye on these cookies! They are sooooo tasty. I hope you enjoy them as much as I do.

Cut Out Cookie Glaze

2 cups Confectioners or Powdered Sugar

4 tsp light corn syrup

4 tsp dairy free milk (start with 2tsp and add as needed)

Food color as desired

Mix sugar, corn syrup and dairy free milk thoroughly.
Add food coloring if you wish to add color to the glaze.
Spread over cooled cookies. It will dry shiny and firm.

Soft and Chewy Sugar Cookies

These cookies are really tasty and chewy. They almost melt in your mouth!

12 tbsp dairy free margarine, softened

1 ½ cup sugar

2 cups flour

½ tsp baking powder

½ tsp salt

Egg replacer + water to replace 1 egg (follow directions on box)

1 tsp vanilla

½ cup sugar to roll cookies in

Preheat oven to 350°

With a hand or stand mixer, blend sugar and dairy free margarine together until smooth in a large bowl. Add in egg replacer + water for 1 egg and keep mixing.

In a medium bowl, stir together flour, salt, baking powder and vanilla.

Slowly incorporate the flour mixture into the wet mixture until all ingredients are well combined.

Pour sugar into a small bowl.

Take a small scoop of dough and roll into a ball, then roll around in sugar and place onto greased or parchment paper lined cookie sheet. Slightly press down cookie on sheet and bake them for 8 to 10 minutes until lightly browned around edges. Remove from oven and let sit for about 5 minutes before moving to cooling rack.

Enjoy.

Sugar Cookie Fruit Pizza

Sugar Cookie Crust- follow recipe for soft and chewy sugar cookies, page 138

8 oz package dairy free cream cheese, softened

¾ cup sugar

2 tbsp frozen orange juice concentrate, optional

1 cup dairy free whipped cream, recipe on page 109

Preheat oven to 350°

Place sugar cookie dough onto pizza stone or into a jelly roll pan lined with parchment paper.

Bake for 10-12 minutes or until lightly browned.

Let cool.

With a mixer blend dairy free cream cheese and sugar until creamy. Add orange juice concentrate if desired and blend. Fold in dairy free whipped cream until all is combined.

Spread mixture over cooled cookie crust. Layer fruit of your choice all over pizza. Place in fridge to cool for at least one hour. Serve and enjoy.

Brownies

I have been on a long hunt for an allergy friendly brownie and this one is a mixture of a few recipes and it tastes fantastic! They have a nice crisp top and a chewy chocolately inside. Enjoy.

½ cup sugar

2 tbsp dairy free margarine

2 tbsp water

1 ½ cup allergy friendly chocolate chips

½ tsp salt

2/3 cup flour

¼ tsp baking soda

½ tsp vanilla

½ cup unsweetened applesauce

Preheat the oven to 325°

Take a little pat of dairy free margarine and grease an 8x8 in pan with it. I like to use the dairy free margarine not cooking spray. I find the cooking spray makes the brownies turn out oily and hard.

In a large bowl, stir together the flour, salt and baking soda. Set aside.

In a saucepan over medium heat bring the water, sugar and dairy free margarine to a boil. Stir ingredients until mixture is smooth and then remove it from the heat. Pour in the chocolate chips and stir until they are well combined.

Add the unsweetened applesauce and vanilla and stir. Pour the chocolate mixture into the flour mixture and stir until all ingredients are combined.

Pour into the pan and bake for 25-30 minutes. Do Not Overbake. Brownies are done when a toothpick inserted into the middle comes out clean.

Sponge Candy

Now I know this may seem intimidating, but you can definitely do this!! This is a candy that my son always wants to try, so I said Let's do this!! And it is sooooo worth it!! It is really unique and delicious!

And a Buffalo, NY food group. Haha

¼ tsp gelatin

1 tsp water

1 ½ cups sugar

½ cups light corn syrup

½ cup water

1 tbsp baking soda

Put 1 tsp of water in a small bowl and scatter the gelatin over the water and set it aside.

Line a 9x9 pan or spring form pan with parchment paper.

Now take a pot with tall sides on it and place the sugar, water and corn syrup on medium heat. I like to stir it with a wooden spoon until all the sugar breaks down and it is a smooth consistency. Bring it to a boil and place a candy thermometer in the pot and stop stirring! Bring the sugar mixture to 310°F which takes about 10 minutes.

Take it off the heat and let it set for 5 minutes. The first couple times I made this candy I didn't let it sit long enough and the candy did not come out with that airy goodness. If you add the baking soda when the mixture is too hot it won't rise like it should.

Now add the gelatin mixture and whisk. Then sift the baking soda over the pot and whisk like crazy. This is also important so that the baking soda doesn't clump and your candy will taste like sponge candy and not baking soda.

Place the pot back on the heat and whisk for 30 seconds and the candy will rise high in the pot. This is it, pure success!!

Pour the mixture into your pan and let it go. Don't spread it around or make it look pretty. That will cause the candy to deflate and you won't get your airy goodness in the candy.

Let it sit for about 2 to 3 hours to harden. Then chop all of it up as best you can. This is a tricky and very messy step!

Melt dairy free chocolate and dip the candy pieces into it and let it dry.

Also I like to add 1 tsp of orange extract to melted chocolate to make Orange Sponge Candy, which is worth every little calorie.

Enjoy and be brave! You can do this.

Perfect Pie Crust

2 cups sifted all-purpose flour

1 tsp salt

2/3 cup shortening

5 to 7 tbsp cold water

Sift together the flour and salt.

Cut the shortening into squares and blend them in with a fork to get the mixture looking like a bowl of tiny pea sized balls.

Then add 1 tbsp of water at a time into the flour mixture until all the dough is moistened. Just make sure that you don't over stir because then your dough may come out tough, you want it to be light and flaky!

Form the dough into a ball and place in the fridge to set.

When you are ready to make the pie, remove the dough ball from the fridge and roll it out.

This amount of dough is enough to make a 9 in double crust pie or 6-8 tart shells.

Fill Crust with desired filling and bake at 400° for about 50 minutes

Non Dairy Sweetened Condensed Milk

3 cups of non-dairy milk

½ cup sugar

Pinch of salt

1 tsp vanilla

Pour milk and sugar into a pan and let it come to a boil, not a rolling boil, more like a simmer.

Let that go until it is reduced to about half. That will take about 1 hour.

Remove from heat.

Cool slightly and stir in salt and vanilla.

The mixture will thicken as it cools

Allow to cool completely and add to your favorite recipe!!

This can last up to one week in the fridge.

Magic Bars

These are one of my son's absolute favorite desserts!! They are delicious!

6 tbsp melted dairy free margarine

1 cup graham cracker crumbs –allergy friendly of your choice

1 cup dairy free chocolate chips

1 cup crispy rice cereal (optional) - sometimes I like them in, sometimes I like them out! It depends on your crunchy mood

1 cup flaked coconut

12 oz dairy free sweetened condensed milk, found on page 148

Preheat oven to 350°

Pour melted dairy free margarine into 9x13 pan

Sprinkle graham cracker crumbs over margarine

Then take the other ingredients and layer them on the bars. Do not ever stir this mixture, just layer.

Start with the dairy free chocolate chips and spread them across the pan, then the cereal, and coconut.

Finally pour the dairy free sweetened condensed milk all over ingredients and place in oven for 25 minutes or until golden brown and bubbly.

Allow to cool completely before cutting into squares. Yummy.

Dessert Pizza

This is a recipe I used to eat all the time at my friend Margaret's house for sleepovers! It is so good and brings back a lot of really great memories and it converts beautifully to being allergy friendly. Enjoy.

½ cup shortening

½ cup peanut free spread (I like to use a sunflower seed spread)

½ cup brown sugar

½ cup sugar

Egg replacer equivalent to 2 eggs—3 tsp powder and 4 tbsp warm water

½ tsp vanilla extract

1 ½ cups flour

2 cups mini marshmallows

1 cup dairy free chocolate chips

Preheat oven to 375°

In a small bowl whisk the egg replacer and water. Whip it until it's foamy.

In a large bowl, blend the peanut free spread, shortening and sugars until creamy.

Pour in the egg replacer mixture and vanilla. Beat that until all is combined

Slowly incorporate the flour until a smooth dough forms.

Next take a greased pizza pan and spread the mixture out onto the pan.

Bake pizza for 12 minutes and remove from the oven.

Now take the marshmallows and dairy free chocolate chips and cover the entire pizza. Put it back in the oven to melt and brown the pizza. This should take about 3-5 minutes. Make sure you watch it so it doesn't burn. Enjoy the warm ooey gooey goodness. Yummy.

Chocolate Peanutless Butter Pie

1 nine-inch unbaked pie crust. (A lot of brands are actually allergy friendly)

Chocolate Filling:

½ cup dairy free margarine, softened

½ cup sugar

Egg replacer +water to replace 1 egg

¾ cup dairy free chocolate chips, melted

¾ cup vanilla extract

Preheat oven to 450°. Bake pie crust for 9 to 11 minutes. Cool.

Chocolate Filling:

In a small bowl blend egg replacer+ water and blend until frothy. Set aside.

In a medium bowl, blend dairy free margarine and sugar until creamy. Add applesauce and mix. Pour in dairy free chocolate and vanilla and mix until well combined.

Smooth 1 cup of the mixture over the cooled crust and let it sit aside.

"Peanutless Butter" Filling

8 oz dairy free cream cheese, softened

½ cup Peanut free spread. (I use a sunflower seed spread)

1 cup powdered sugar

Egg replacer +water to replace 1 egg

1 ½ cups dairy free whipped cream, recipe on page 109

"Peanutless Butter" Filling:

Place egg replacer and water in a small bowl and blend until frothy. Set aside.

Mix the peanut free spread and the dairy free cream cheese together until well combined. I use a hand mixer on medium speed. Add in the powdered sugar and egg replacer and water and mix until creamy. Then slowly incorporate the dairy free whipped cream into the mix. Just stir the cream in, do not use the blender.

Dollop the Peanutless Butter filling in batches over the chocolate filling. Take a spatula and smoosh it all over until you have created an even layer over the chocolate layer. Now spread the rest of the chocolate layer over the top.

Place in fridge to cool and set until ready to serve.

This is so creamy and delicious.

Index

Cinnamon

Chicken

Chocolate

Milkshake

Made in the USA
Charleston, SC
27 October 2014